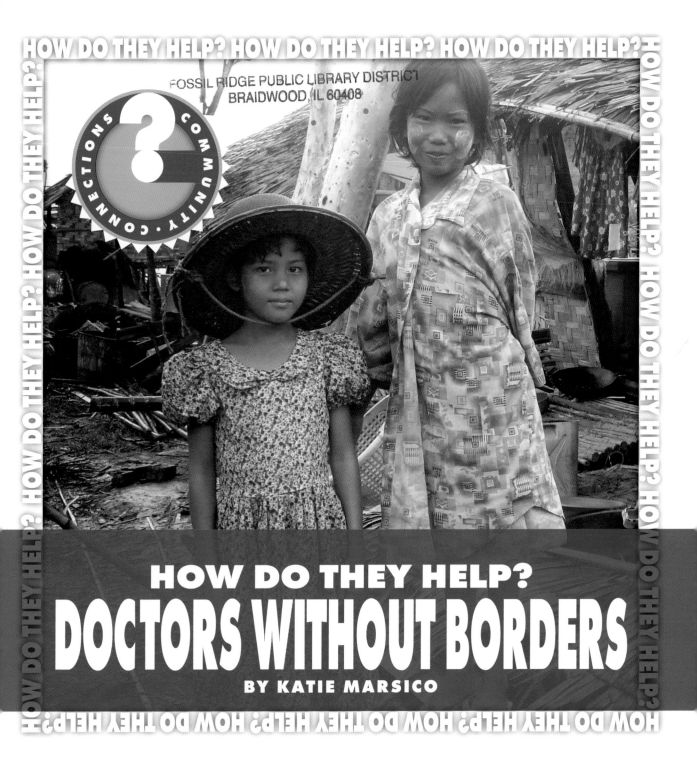

COMMUNITY · CONNECTIONS

HOW DO THEY HELP?
DOCTORS WITHOUT BORDERS
BY KATIE MARSICO

Published in the United States of America by Cherry Lake Publishing
Ann Arbor, Michigan
www.cherrylakepublishing.com

Content Adviser: Cynthia Rathinasamy, Master of Public Policy, Concentration in
International Development, Gerald R. Ford School of Public Policy,
The University of Michigan, Ann Arbor, MI
Reading Adviser: Marla Conn, ReadAbility, Inc.

Photo Credits: © lakareutangranser/www.flickr.com/CC BY-SA 2.0, cover, 1, 11; © Dragon
Images/Shutterstock Images, 5; © Daniel Alvarez/Shutterstock Images, 7; © Julien Harneis/
www.flickr.com/ CC BY-SA 2.0, 9; © Arjun Claire/www.flickr.com/CC BY 2.0, 13;
© Tom Skrinar//www.flickr.com/ CC BY-SA 2.0, 15, 19; © Jason Taellious/www.flickr.com/
CC BY-SA 2.0, 17; © Shyamalamuralinath/Shutterstock Images, 21

LIBRARY OF CONGRESS CATALOGING-IN-PUBLICATION DATA
Marsico, Katie, 1980-
  Doctors without Borders / by Katie Marsico.
    pages cm. — (Community connections)
  Includes bibliographical references and index.
  ISBN 978-1-63188-027-8 (hardcover) — ISBN 978-1-63188-113-8 (pdf) —
ISBN 978-1-63188-070-4 (pbk.) — ISBN 978-1-63188-156-5 (ebook)
  1. Medical assistance–Developing countries–Juvenile literature. 2. Midecins sans frontihres
(Association)–Juvenile literature. 3. International relief–Developing countries–Juvenile literature.
  [1. Doctors without Borders (Association)] I. Title.
  RA390.F8M37 2015
  362.1'0425091724—dc23   2014006219

Cherry Lake Publishing would like to acknowledge the
work of The Partnership for 21st Century Skills. Please
visit www.p21.org for more information.

Printed in the United States of America
Corporate Graphics Inc.

Note to Reader: Doctors Without Borders was founded by the French.
The French name is Médecins Sans Frontières.
The group also uses MSF as its acronym.

CONTENTS

SUPPORTING SURVIVAL

People living in the West African nation of Mali are often poor. Many don't receive basic medical care. **Malnutrition**, diseases, and **epidemics** are common. Children are especially in danger. For every 1,000 children born in Mali, only 178 will live to the age of five.

A vaccination is a shot or drops taken by mouth that prevent people from getting a disease.

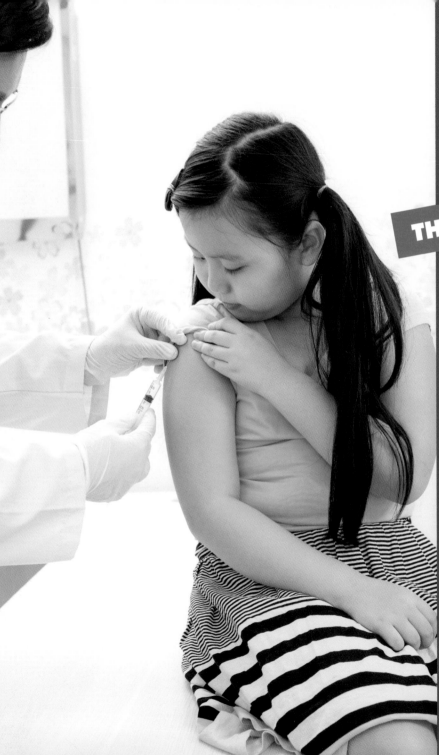

THINK!

Think about how often you visit the doctor. Do you get vaccinations? How about medicine when you're sick? What do you think would happen to you if you didn't get vaccinations or medicine?

5

Fortunately, Doctors Without Borders is helping. This group provides people living in Mali with food, drugs, and medical treatment.

Doctors Without Borders gives emergency medical **aid** to millions of people in almost 70 countries. War, poverty, and natural disaster keep these people from getting basic health care.

The doctors and nurses in the group also give checkups and information about how to stop the

People in poor areas like this one in Haiti might not be able to see a local doctor.

Can you guess what *poverty* means? If you answered "the state of being poor," you'd be right. How does being poor affect health?

7

spread of disease. Sometimes they perform surgeries. They also provide people with food, water, medicine, and other items that support safety and wellness.

Doctors Without Borders does not get involved with the reasons why people need aid. The workers never deny patients medical services because of their backgrounds or beliefs. The group tells other organizations about people who are suffering or living without medical care.

When doctors help sick people become healthy, the whole community improves.

LOOK!

Go online with a parent or teacher. Look for pictures of Doctors Without Borders helping others. What kind of medical care do you see the workers providing? How are they helping different communities around the world?

WORKING BEYOND BOUNDARIES

The idea for Doctors Without Borders started during a war in Nigeria. Between 1967 and 1970, the French Red Cross asked volunteers to go to this West African nation to help people suffering from hunger, illnesses, and injuries.

French doctors soon realized that troops often attacked innocent people. Children starved because

Doctors Without Borders helps storm victims.

LOOK!

Look at this picture of Myanmar. This area has been affected by extreme weather. What medical aid do you think people living here need? What other services would help this community recover?

11

the military wouldn't let food and supplies pass across enemy lines.

French doctors realized that most of the world didn't know what was happening in Nigeria. Meanwhile, in southern Asia, flooding had created medical emergencies. Journalists, or reporters, knew this but felt that the world was unaware. The two groups joined together and started Doctors Without Borders in 1971.

Doctors Without Borders tries to help anyone who needs it. This includes people affected by war.

Think about the challenges these health care workers must overcome. They travel to war zones where people are injured by bullets, bombs, and other weapons. Sometimes they offer help in remote areas where it's difficult to regularly communicate with the outside world.

13

Doctors Without Borders workers come from countries across the globe. Every day, almost 30,000 of these men and women deliver emergency medical aid.

Doctors and nurses do some of the jobs. **Counselors**, scientists, and plumbing and electrical experts do other work. They usually earn a small monthly salary.

Doctors Without Borders include workers with many different skills.

MAKE A GUESS!

Try to guess how Doctors Without Borders pays for the aid it provides. You'd be right if you said it gets *some* help from national governments. Yet more than four-fifths of the group's funding comes from private **donations**.

15

SEVERAL IMPORTANT SERVICES

Workers sometimes see patients in permanent buildings such as hospitals and clinics. In other cases, they offer medical services in tents or temporary health centers. These doctors and nurses treat everything from gun and knife wounds to measles and malnutrition.

Medical care doesn't have to be given in building.

Doctors Without Borders treats cholera and meningitis. Workers also treat human immunodeficiency virus (HIV)/acquired immunodeficiency syndrome (AIDS). Find out what health problems all of these cause if left untreated.

17

Workers often deal with life-threatening problems and **crises**. Yet they also provide vaccinations and checkups to children and to women who are expecting babies.

Mental health services are also offered by Doctors Without Borders. Counselors help victims of violence and disaster understand and deal with their feelings. The group donates food,

Physical and mental health care are both very important to keep a community strong.

ASK QUESTIONS!

How else does war
affect civilians? What
dangers do they face?
Are they at added
risk for certain health
problems?

19

water, blankets, and cooking pots to struggling communities. Workers help rebuild hospitals and develop more modern health care programs.

Some communities have been ignored by their own government or are affected by violence.

Doctors Without Borders helps raise awareness about the health and safety issues they face. Thanks to this group's efforts, fewer people suffer in silence.

Maybe this child will grow up to join Doctors Without Borders. Or maybe you will!

You can help spread the word about communities that are struggling with health care emergencies. Create posters that describe some of these situations. Ask people around your community— including local doctors and nurses— to hang the posters in their offices.

GLOSSARY

aid (AYDE) food, money, or other goods and services given to people in need

counselors (KAUNT-suhl-uhrz) workers who provide guidance and advice that support emotional health

crises (KRY-seez) difficult or dangerous situations that usually require immediate attention

donations (doh-NAY-shuhnz) money, food, clothes, or other items that are given to help someone in need

epidemics (ep-i-DEM-iks) illnesses affecting a large number of people at the same time in the same area

malnutrition (mal-noo-TRIH-shuhn) a sick or weak state caused by not eating enough healthy food

remote (ree-MOWT) far away from cities and other communities

FIND OUT MORE

BOOKS

Hand, Carol. *Vaccines*. Minneapolis: ABDO Publishing Company, 2013.

Person, Stephen. *Malaria: Super Killer!* New York: Bearport Publishing, 2011.

Senker, Cath. *Poverty and Hunger*. Mankato, MN: Smart Apple Media, 2012.

WEB SITES

National Geographic Kids—Malaria Is Still a Problem in Africa

kids.nationalgeographic.com/kids/stories/spacescience/malaria
Head to this Web site for additional information about malaria and how to prevent it.

TeensHealth—Hunger and Malnutrition

kidshealth.org/teen/food_fitness/nutrition/hunger.html
Check out this Web page to learn more about how these conditions affect kids' health.

INDEX

ABOUT THE AUTHOR

Katie Marsico is the author of more than 150 children's books. She lives in a suburb of Chicago, Illinois, with her husband and children.